Gibel Carps, Dog Parks, and Midnight Moons

Gibel Carps, Dog Parks, and Midnight Moons

Miracles of the Sky

DIAN CUNNINGHAM PARROTTA

RESOURCE *Publications* • Eugene, Oregon

GIBEL CARPS, DOG PARKS, AND MIDNIGHT MOONS
Miracles of the Sky

Copyright © 2020 Dian Cunningham Parrotta. All rights reserved. Except for brief quotations in critical publications or reviews, no part of this book may be reproduced in any manner without prior written permission from the publisher. Write: Permissions, Wipf and Stock Publishers, 199 W. 8th Ave., Suite 3, Eugene, OR 97401.

Resource Publications
An Imprint of Wipf and Stock Publishers
199 W. 8th Ave., Suite 3
Eugene, OR 97401

www.wipfandstock.com

PAPERBACK ISBN: 978-1-7252-7065-7
HARDCOVER ISBN: 978-1-7252-7066-4
EBOOK ISBN: 978-1-7252-7067-1

Manufactured in the U.S.A. 06/10/20

in memory of my two english bullies, jimmy mateo and simon the crusader, whose spirits returned to the blessed sky often showing me themselves in huge floating clouds always still following me around

FUNERAL BLUES

Stop all the clocks, cut off the telephone, Prevent the dog from barking with a juicy bone, Silence the pianos and with muffled drum Bring out the coffin, let the mourners come. Let aeroplanes circle moaning overhead Scribbling on the sky the message He is Dead. Put crepe bows round the white necks of the public doves, Let the traffic policemen wear black cotton gloves. He was my North, my South, my East and West, my working week and my Sunday rest, my noon, my midnight, my talk, my song; I thought that love would last forever: I was wrong. The stars are not wanted now; put out everyone, pack up the moon and dismantle the sun, Pour away the ocean and sweep up the woods; For nothing now can ever come to any good.

W.H. AUDEN

JIMMY MY BRINDLE BRIGHT

my brindle bull dog's
face was my sun and he shone
a luminous glow

my brownish tawny
my piebald bully, jimmy
my dog star you know

SIMON MY BIG HUGHEY BABY IN DIAPERS ALWAYS MY HEART

my white simon the
crusader in cloth diapers
my little baby

no not a lap dog
simon, nope, didn't know that
he's my velcro dog

CONTENTS

prose poetry	1
a dog park in the sky	2
ode to the sky's falling	3
a sky double dream	4
against a cloudy winter's starling sky	5
i hear a cloud drumming a tatt-tatt tattooing	6
flashing spirit lights inside my eyes' sky	7
a white winter sky	9
humble puddles capture the great gorgeous sky	10
see stormy sea	11
big sky park	12
rainbow warrior's cloudy serenade	13
in the lavapies quarter of madrid	14
a floating sabot cloud and water dolphins	15
authentic italian focaccia bread clouds	16
the sun light's reflection	17
ghost-ridden hunchback whale clouds	18
our night sky with moru misa rattle moons	19
a parabola sky	20
a found sunset bird sky	21
haibun poetry	22
Under the Coney Island Sky	23
seagulls' breath	24
night sky	25
new york city sky	26
a sky double dream	27
ekphrastic poetry	28

ekphrasis poem tribute to giselle (royal opera ballet): under the midnight moons	29
a windy oil painted sky: ekphrasis poem tribute to georgia o'keeffe	30
haiku poetry	31
miracle of the sun haikus	32
miracle of fatima	33
the most exceptional aurora borealis twenty years later	34
this phenomenon perceived in most countries	35
exceptional intensity for these latitudes	36
the sky was aflame with a strange glow: a crimson cloud	37
towards the zenith	38
sun's vivid blood-red glow	39
midnight moon haikus: those waxing waning moons	40
selene	41
the night full mooncake haiku	42
choppy sea cloud haikus	43
a sharp coastal sky haikus	44
tanka poems	45
tanka poems about the night and the night-time sky	46

PROSE POETRY

an essential book to have on your shelf is "the rose metal press field guide to prose poetry" edited by gary l. mcdowell and f. daniel rzicznek and read the chapter called "ticking the box: the rules and permissions of the prose poem form is a real useful chapter if you would like to learn how to contain your poetry into this well-ordered airtight tupperware canisters so square plumb rectangular or square tiny boxed in and true to stack on tall with snap close lids do capture your images into neat storage vessels

A DOG PARK IN THE SKY

in acts 1:9 the text says *that when Jesus ascended into Heaven, that:*
"a cloud *received him out of their sight."*

in verse 11—two angels stood there telling the disciples that Jesus would:
"come in like manner as ye have seen him go into heaven."
which means with clouds!

clouds pounding my heartache away when I see the flying coney island gulls in my virginia's early morning winter sky is a powerful madeleine of growing up brooklyn days again where my mom, dad, grandma tess and aunt mary lou were never too far away to hug and then there are the two dog clouds my canine companions nearby running upside down. trees. grass. snow. there's a dog park in my sky with a notorious winter breeze crafting a now comfort of nimbus shapes of my beloved best friend buddies spreading out inside of those cumulus clouds' stocky a bulking up more muscular folds of floating shrouds with those short cut tails slapping upward still always there following me.

ODE TO THE SKY'S FALLING

"the only constant is change," (heraclitus) but isn't there a beauty in the letting go various shades of two by two colors like yellow-orange those slivered slices of the warm colors of sun or fire then there's the cool colors calm soothing recede making those spaces seem larger think calming blue waters through violets and gray greens. those falling leaves in a brilliant show from red, yellow to orange to bronze to browns of dried herbs of peppermint leaves, lavender, chamomile, borage, caraway and catnip from sunlight to cool nights of feallan that falling down autumn's phase of ripeness before winter's old age dies like in a dripping candle clock or in western europe's in prague's times striking inside of that astronomical clock with an allegorical parade of animated sculpture rings on the hour every day. look at autumn's equinox and the pair of balance scales of libra represented by an inanimate, that sign of justice, balance and harmony of the creeping barrage in our gigantic empty space of our ephemeral universe but bringing the unchanging that fifth element, the only constant that does not change that stereotype of our epitome of a calm a perpetual and eternal unvarying. keep and hold on tightly to the quintessence of your calm like even believe you are really on a magical carpet ride and never let it land low or stop flying cause you can body rocket in the summer sky is the constellation that sagittarius *hasits* handle on the left and you showjumping low into space rides and fly indigo around milky way appears as steam out the spout of the teapot falling

A SKY DOUBLE DREAM

like look up into an overgrown pond upon slender-bodied fish with bright crisp jupiter with white the sparkle chinese gibel carp with molar pharyngeal throat teeth and just below is its partner that yellow-orange comet goldfish hanging with the black moor with scales are velvety that's glistening venus. see the telescope and bubble eyes of shiny feldspar mica sparkly with brightly colored fish flank scales are silvery turquoise, red-brown spots of rainbow purples, greens, browns and filmy pellicle scums like microscopic fungi with sagittarius' forced fan-like flapping filaments and voids. there's a benmoreite volcanic rock wall wrapped across the sky like robotic appendages of dragons' teeth and giants' tooth-structures harden heavy like lava formations on a moving crystal plate below to the south, its silence bulging out of a vertical girdled chain-linked oak tree floating like driftwood. my walrus body holds its foreflippers close my body swims through star clusters, nebulae with wisps of outpouring gases glowing and rubble as big as small moons and inside frozen oort clouds icy swimming flat-faced above stretches of space containing galactic crab nebula inside of supercluster day dreaming where the archipelagoes like little dots scattered zooming in below so teeming with astonishing blue majestic whales, unicorn narwhals herds led by my two floating bull dogs with sunning satisfied smiles propelled by my false awakening from a dream within a dream

AGAINST A CLOUDY WINTER'S STARLING SKY

at a moments' notice on the edge with twisting spectacle changes in directions of a swooping into that unpredictability of their intricately coordinated patterns those eerier flocks of hundreds of thousands of starlings fly in fast-moving cloud formations through ascent and push forming funnels into a flanking line with a velum edge of a thin layer of semilunar shapes collapse into a quick shift with momentum on a wave suggestively a hitchcock-dark a supernatural shapeshifting with fantastical speed causing a collision between air earth waves' swell seismic hums that nobody hears a murmuration that swooping mass they gather over their roosting sites preferring urban artificial structures on power lines, telephone wires or on a monumental mass or tapering towers or on pylons keeping a closeness a warm cozy at night

I HEAR A CLOUD DRUMMING A TATT-TATT TATTOOING

a pileated woodpecker with a long neck with a flaming-red triangular crest curves a black with brave bleached those white stripes a PIE-lee-ay-tid, or a PILL-ee-ay-tid woodpecker pecks a drumming fixed algorithm heard inside my head a tatt-tatt tatting—da da da da da da a heart-beat a beating thick tic tic tic a pileated peckers' tree knocking tock a mysterious a scintillating tap tok tok a pounding beat a balanced weary a level calming that sensible discerning a nurturing patter rhythming a cue to pursue one's unique pulse-pitch rapping out aloud
a cloud over head
a pileated woodpecker
heard inside my head

FLASHING SPIRIT LIGHTS INSIDE MY EYES' SKY

eyeball rubbing inside of the dark than those colorful swirls to those diaphanous wings that sore around the whirring hive a so stronger then it appears like bees going rogue with billions of multi-colored dots like tiny spots shimmering overcrowded spec smog swarm a fuzz-hiss horde-dance huddling above a bevy of thousands and it's sounding like a mantra in my mind considering one fleck at a time those colored thin sticks of pick-up sticks floating and tiddlywink flips winks then those flying pieces of soft shiny color form plastics in dark colorful trailing floaters out there the noctilucent phosphenes like was just whacked on the head with a brick you see star sparkles, light spirit energies, and orb flashes a wide kaleidoscope of small whirlpool air eddies inside the eyes' closed or open in the night time murky

A WHITE WINTER SKY

sharon, the sky beautifier, from night to dawn from winter to spring but now bare winter branches of my rose of sharon tree stands like an artificial decorative sculpture centerpiece showing ribbed spokes of three or four or more ligaments hanging loosely like an abandoned unclothed umbrella carcasses disjointed by invisible pins with dried seed-pod-lobe packs stuck on branch tips stuffing flowery punches of many white rose blooms. dormant woody tree-bough silhouettes of cold steel shapes those wind mauled ribs of tree branchlets of bare-bones naked stretching stark in the dead of winter still silently always ornamenting furrows and ruts sometimes snow covered white tree outline the pinks and blue skies'pastels sometimes dotted with nighttime midnight moons and star dots on its branch tips lighted magic fire sticks dazzling

HUMBLE PUDDLES CAPTURE THE GREAT GORGEOUS SKY

see the great sky inside the wet brick road puddle reflections like a big picture window. those colors of grey whites and woody browns the bare tree limbs outstretched on streets with the blues captured inside amazing photo poetry and puddle grams with mobile photography with uninterrupted glass-like surfaces creating symmetry copying stunning compositions onto the seemingly invisible planes like how shadows and reflections show-stop-slip away wordlessly by lights that shape cast on surfaces that sheen those natural, artificial and those street lights

SEE STORMY SEA

see these pure grays these fork-tailed stormy petrels opinionated seabirds splash against the squally sky absquatulate with long hanging legs discombobulated wide outstretched water sorceresses with wide wings seemingly pompous know-all's but how they do cry the incoming gales of unheard warnings to the scattering white sails with rising water waves, blowing clouds and winds keeping bows plowing through massive waves striking towering walls of water swell a brininess of wild fish odor so sulfurous stale funky wheeling in cries of gulls flying inside dense dark tubular low roll horizontals a menacing mischievousness

BIG SKY PARK

squadron of dusty dogs run by when the llama wearing a very long great egret tall on top of its head but it could be an endangered whooping crane with its outstretched neck both piggybacking next to that fat white cow floating the fair-weather cumulus cloud mounds fluctuating in the sky all come sweeping past like a flotilla coastal cruising grounds soaking up atmosphere. so they all anchor above the rich turquoise blue and sailing southward slow, maneuvering between me and the loyal labrador by the dog park gate while that afador-airedale terrier mixed breed, and afghan hound are chased. that champion sprinter of dogdom there those dark-eyed small-eared greyhound there having bloodlines traceable back through irish sires the fastest of all dogs running at full gallop here at benjamin banneker off-leash dog park playtime under open clouded skies' twilight soon after sunset so illuminating

RAINBOW WARRIOR'S CLOUDY SERENADE

altostratus cloud formations of a sad elder maybe brave Lakota head of the afterworld his thickened image into storm clouds erupting rain-bearing nimbostratus a shadowy figure wearing a headdress war bonnet with big flat nose with an unexpressive face with dull eyes with opaque eagle feathers with falling lightning bolts, electrical then thunder sounds between the cloud-to-ground some brilliant flashes iridescent across the yellow-orange-red green, blue, indigo and violet's the end of the spectrum scattering the light blue hues outwards a quick-moving-double-rainbow conduits rustling through the rushing rain then a pit-pat a splittering of more drops a cloudy serenade hard against the back of my house windows

IN THE LAVAPIES QUARTER OF MADRID

how the arm movement strong and dominant a lot of flamenco dancing in madrid's casa patas lets you feel your inner duende magical nights taking flamenco very seriously in a darkened 9-midnight moon lighted-room-like under a darkened evening sky. there an old black baile hand-clapping percussive footwork flamenco dancer dances the movement of the smooth & elegant arms, hands & fingers giving grace & magic to the dance together with the contoneo of the body communication of feelings that each move possesses joy, sensuality, sadnesses, and passions always above the waist inside called canizres with santiago cake with almonds & toast with ensaladilla with scrambled green eggs & ham with casa patas ratatouille & sliced jamon iberico de bellota, the rich flavored cured run free acorn-fed Iberico pig. the old woman black dancer can turn on a pin round and round a completely upright spin next to the cast-iron columns painted dark green those people at the small tables in chairs eating, drinking, hand clapping, emotional movements & facial expressions with magnetism & charming oomph of folkloric charms of the roma people of andalusia

A FLOATING SABOT CLOUD AND WATER DOLPHINS

a weighty sabot like a clunky inside that cloud a floating block of wood or a crusty ciabatta like a wooden shoe, a clog, a wind-driven sky-cloud rests spirits and charms the mind while watching it roll in then collapsing on the glide like folklore klompendansen in the netherlands in the streets with the klompen dancers with high kicks in wooden clogs dance insoles made from ash wood, tapping toes with moving ankles and heels on wood in the streets at tulip time festival but now in the sky outside my window that moving sky festival of quaint villages, windmills flowers, fish and cheese, runaway rosters and brooding hens with men in boats fishing in turbid in brackish waters those most plentiful of orange-golden carp fish swilling side-way flops porpoise out of lakes and so slow-moving impressive

AUTHENTIC ITALIAN FOCACCIA BREAD CLOUDS

there were clouds inside of her spaghetti pots grandma tessy's kneaded soft floating gummy sponge dough full with wet that flour and yeast upside down spilling out of a grey rim of a mid-century revere ware, her old stock pots, cookware spilling out stratus flour onto a cloud glass cutting board sky with white hollow cumulonimbus tumultuous blessed messy banquet floury focaccia rising doubling under tea-towels dusted and thumb dimpled extra-virgin-olive oiled white surface & 2 teaspoon pinches of flakey sea and garlic salts bleu or asiago an Italian cheesy, and dried rosemary smooth that plasticity of white doughy clouds floating nice and airy elasticities of hope as the flying swallow bird sings his twitter-warble song with a long mechanical-sounding whirrs followed by that chirp

THE SUN LIGHT'S REFLECTION

a five-petaled like a growing periwinkle dancing on a white wall like a glossy a purple-bluish ornamental faint dim a jewel with its light scattering a pool of shuddering wings is just magical as standing center stage a yellow sprite as an amber glowing incandescent shadows & softly broken a silvery cluster of a pirouette a rotation or spinning to orchestra strings so harmonies are thick and lush with a nice interplay of a delicate glow of fading rays dancing on a surface smooth and shiny like floating tranquil ripples waving waves those painted strokes on a watercolor mountain range so gorgeous

GHOST-RIDDEN HUNCHBACK WHALE CLOUDS

hunchbacks breach a mirage a distorted elongated horizontal a flat shoreline like a ghost mountain blocking the sound those low-lying dark storm clouds that hang imitate breaching whales picking up speed near the water leaping way above its surface falling a whale lying on its side raises a long their pectoral fins slap into the air and slamming back to the surface smacking and those the tern petrels spreading their plumes, mantling arching shoulders with there's that spouting & fluking in synchrony then the lots of anchovies, the splash of vertical shadows of dinner mint-pink and yellow-green light camouflage shadows through bioluminescent glow, the light-shrimp krill and plankton, mackerel, capelin, those cormorants and gulls majestically all caress the flat shoreline mouth kissing swarms smelling hunchback whales' breath

OUR NIGHT SKY WITH MORU MISA RATTLE MOONS

is the beautiful Jarawa's natives of buka and bougainville at northern solomon islands in melanesia and chopi people of mozambique in southwest coast of africa natives of bougainville, papua new guinea, that tribal music of southern sudan at social and ceremonial gathers have shuffling in single file twinkling of legs outside villages under shade trees those rolling rumps & the five drums & horns & music & rhythms the vessel rattles like midnight moons made from small gourd plants dried filled with stones & okra & sorghum seeds sealed up with cassava leaves a spherical body and narrow tapering neck a smooth yellowish orange the moru misa rattle gara with men dancing in outer circle and women inner circles their black skins oiled and glistening with women's hair the stars shining against powerful shoulders the drumming, dancing RUMA and singing till turning a slate grey in the rising sun

A PARABOLA SKY

asymmetrical open plane curve like a fixed straight line the directrix like a banana cloud floating an upside-down U and a rainbow forms behind elegant geometric forms the sun peeks out through the graceful arch of steel suspension-cables of the brooklyn bridge with those mile-high ghostly shadowy mind mirages where the twin towers were then the water fountain spouts spurting upward from this city's water fountain's splashing up into the hot of summer spreading upward out into a parabola sky against the arts and architecture of new york city's abstract blows layered blends of rows of lights against its canopy of downtown skyscrapers, cityscapes of a heavy white/grey

A FOUND SUNSET BIRD SKY

the newly bought thrift shop find of an acrylic framed painting of flying sunset birds of all kinds on rose-lavender with single branch with hanging leaf a silhouette of an american bird sky with swifts congregating in a communal roost in a so artificial chimney tower. there's those eastern nightjars whip-poor-will and chuck-will's-widow with long, slender wings and see the wilson's snip cheery-up, cheery-oh with the woodcock's peent callers shattering with spiraling wings twittering brush strokes animating feathers' zips darts simulating movements of an artist's brush capturing wings flying a high west sunset

HAIBUN POETRY

this is a prose poem with a haiku at the beginning or the end of the piece. it helps move the story forward taking the narrative in another direction. prose in the haibun tells the story while the haiku puts a spotlight on the its theme, mood and tone~

UNDER THE CONEY ISLAND SKY

Tanned, huge-bouncing boobs hanging big with a Marylyn-Monroe-singing-softly-voice, crooning chiseled short sexy trills of *ice-cold orange creamsicles, popsicles, fudgsicles. Gotcha ice cold red, white and blue Rocket ice Pumps Pops. Iced cold cans of coke, root beer, orange sodas. And* gotta Killem, these Ballantine beers *blasts and gots* cigarettes. *Save me, one unsold cold one for Jimmy Gargiulo's my man.* The two wearing yellow-taxi-man Nickel-Plated Steel Money Changers with penny, nickel, dime and quarter barrels, swingin loosely on waistbands, round their bare bellies. Refracting splendid awe-inspiring masterpieces of stained-glass rainbows, scattering, like flying kaleido s c o p i c surfaces tilting against those heated wafting miscellaneous carnival Funnel Cakes, frying burgers, french fries, Coney's Cones whiffing out sugar smoke into a swelteringly against the beach's salty seawater smells. Aww, Coney Island, the buttress, a magical gem, a dreamland I used to know interwoven in the dithering washed out white noise of the vendors' coins mixing with seagulls'
huah huah hu
huah huah huah hu
huah huoh hu

SEAGULLS' BREATH

little old aunt mae, the herman's block-party guest sound like seagulls in her breath when a breeze blows by with her sitting in our alley chair huah huah huah or a smile or a hello heard or shown her way or a child or children pass by bouncing pink spalding balls huah huah huah. when the american flags all blow in the breeze and the screen doors slam screams huah huah huah. when billy geodano turns up the hi-fi when the barbecues coals turn white huah huah huah. when nanna passes by with a plate of food huah huah huah while all four families happily congregate huah huah huah.
how happy this day
among the neighborhood friends
a cherished moment

NIGHT SKY

wild black mustang stallions wrapped and stretch across the night sky in harems of geldings and broodmares fretting fence lines more muscled, more poised and fuller of themselves. they run. see those herd free-rangers into a black-framed view. galloping legs on each side of their bodies in unison-gait speed in the night. a stampede of trailblazers without any sound like the quiet of blood rushing through. that angle between the visible horizon and the north celestial pole and can you see north star as the horses leave rising plumes of black velvet dust, cosmic rays filling interstellar space
 stella polaris
shining intermittently
so unsteadily

NEW YORK CITY SKY

asymmetrical open plane curve like a fixed straight line the directrix like a banana cloud floating an upside-down U and a rainbow forms behind elegant geometric forms the sun peeks out through the graceful arch of steel suspension-cables of the brooklyn bridge with those mile-high ghostly shadowy mind mirages where the twin towers were
the water fountain
spouts a parabola sky
streams spurting upward

A SKY DOUBLE DREAM

like look up into an overgrown pond upon slender-bodied fish with bright crisp Jupiter with white the sparkle chinese gibel carp with molar pharyngeal throat teeth and just below is its partner that yellow-orange comet goldfish hanging with the black moor with scales are velvety that's glistening venus. see the telescope and bubble eyes of shiny feldspar mica sparkly with brightly colored fish flank scales are silvery turquoise, red-brown spots of rainbow purples, greens, browns and filmy pellicle scums like microscopic fungi with sagittarius' forced fan-like flapping filaments and voids. there's a benmoreite volcanic rock wall wrapped across the sky like robotic appendages of dragons' teeth and giants' tooth-structures harden heavy like lava formations on a moving crystal plate below to the south, its silence bulging out of a vertical girdled chain-linked oak tree floating like driftwood. my walrus body holds its foreflippers close my body swims through star clusters, nebulae with wisps of outpouring gases glowing and rubble as big as small moons and inside frozen oort clouds icy swimming flat-faced above stretches of space containing galactic crab nebula inside of supercluster day dreaming where the archipelagoes like little dots scattered zooming

unicorn narwhals
led by two floating bull dogs
dream within a dream

EKPHRASTIC POETRY

ekphrastic poetry celebrates other artists' work and may even intensify and widen its stance~~ by writing about a scene seen in artwork and what did the subjects do after the painting or a poet speaks as a character inside of the painting looking from the inside out or how the artist might have been looking down from an airplane as georgia o'keeffe captures her 'sky above clouds IV' collection was fascinated by looking out of the plane onto the clouded sky or write about how you as the poet's experience is when you see the art piece~~ or how this artist's work has taken you to that next level as anne sexton was so inspired by vincent van gogh's famous painting *starry night* enthused her *'the starry night'* or read percy bysshe shelly, *'on the medusa of leonardo da vinci in the florentine gallery'* or robert browning, *'my last duchess'* or walter de la mare, *'brueghel's winter'* or william carlos williams, *'landscape with the fall of icarus'* or john keats, *'ode on a grecian urn'* or one of my favorites is from the poet rainer maria riike *'archaic torso of apollo'* after viewing an ancient sculpture piece

EKPHRASIS POEM TRIBUTE TO GISELLE (ROYAL OPERA BALLET): UNDER THE MIDNIGHT MOONS

sculptures of fine art beauty in three dimensions like a cast metal and unfired clay tree branch arms outstretching over young shoulders and a ballerina's strong dancer's legs midair muscles in balance overhanging tree brushwood in the evening's lighted sky. *giselle* a masterwork, a peasant girl, who dies of a broken heart. sylph-like movements presents an elegant posture of a ballerina swan's arms forward folding flying down with spacing fingers spread wide and here in my gazebo in the dark just like the kennedy center's circle (mezzanine), the lowest balcony so closest to the stage a quintessential tale of a heartbreaking loss and triumphant forgiveness and here free no tickets required then bamboo's younger shoots in two rows of ghostly spirits of dead girls ditched on their wedding day. the "wili" dancers of twenty corps de ballet dressed in wedding gowns like swans in a lake fly an up and bens lower and lower like with the weight of snow mirror the night-time stars mystical magic in moonlit wood. then the neighbor's back porch lights go bright making white lace waltz turn back into bamboo trees then back again and giselle the pile of fallen branches and bark is engulfed inside of the dancing ghosts. hilarion dances and dances as the wind takes the branches shaking trembling shaking jumping up jerking down dies to his death entwining love and death and i am crying in my night-time yard in the cold of winter on my deck hidden inside the darkened gazebo night

A WINDY OIL PAINTED SKY: EKPHRASIS POEM TRIBUTE TO GEORGIA O'KEEFFE

sky above the clouds a windy-windy morning outside last few leaves twist flapping sounding like bed sheets on a windy white line blowing upwards spreading a georgia o'keeffe's large lively canvases with lots and lots of puffy clouds and blue sky like jumping creek rocks spread out one by one paint washed white thousands similar sized an infinity like visual there looking up on a looking down on from a plane visual makes me visualize me jump hopping like on piano across the sky an up and down giggling slipping on slippery cloud skipping rocks quick flick body flyin skid bounce off the blue and white-washed rock cloud sky surfaces

HAIKU POETRY

"haiku" is a traditional form of japanese poetry that everyone remembers writing three lines first and last have five syllables and the middle line has seven but know some and the lines rarely rhyme and never titled but modernization stretches those rules as I sometimes title my haiku for fun and try not to stretch those 17 syllables though some poets do but "the great four" master haiku poets follow the rules read matsuo basho, kobayaski issa, masaoka shiki and of course yosa buson their work is traditional read by matsuo basho writes *an old silent pond/a frog jumps into the pond,/splash!Silence again.*

MIRACLE OF THE SUN HAIKUS

MIRACLE OF FATIMA

in fatima, portugal
the miracle of the sun
on october 17

THE MOST EXCEPTIONAL AURORA BOREALIS TWENTY YEARS LATER

night of the 25th
natural phenomena
most exceptional

THIS PHENOMENON PERCEIVED IN MOST COUNTRIES

everyone believed
there was a gigantic fire
sky above lit up

EXCEPTIONAL INTENSITY FOR THESE LATITUDES

a blue-ish green glow
pale and pretty, covered sky
north-east to north-west

THE SKY WAS AFLAME WITH A STRANGE GLOW: A CRIMSON CLOUD

sky above lit up
an irregular red vault
pushed by an enchanted breath

TOWARDS THE ZENITH

sun changes color
from blood-red to orange-red
to yellow and soared

SUN'S VIVID BLOOD-RED GLOW

the sky was alight
with edges of white fire
as if the sun were rising

MIDNIGHT MOON HAIKUS: THOSE WAXING WANING MOONS

1
a waxing gibbous
that's less than a full faced moon
that's getting bigger

2
a waning gibbous
that decreasing after full
the moon takes mouth bites

3
brightness on its left
think about the sun's whereabouts
with eastward motion

a goddess symbols
the sinister waxing moons
maiden, mother, crone

shows earth the same face
the dark side of the moon—NOT
drifting from the earth

its surface is dark
the fifth-largest satellite
appears very bright

SELENE

drives across the skies
the daughter of the titans
goddess of the moon

THE NIGHT FULL MOONCAKE HAIKU

snow skin mooncake a
floating round white lotus bloom
those hungry gators

CHOPPY SEA CLOUD HAIKUS

the striking skyscapes
that looks like a choppy sea
so agitated

commonly spotted
rolling north america
chasing thunderstorms

they're so ominous
but they tend to dissipate
those eye-catching clouds

A SHARP COASTAL SKY HAIKUS

so rough and rugged
there those nimbostratus clouds
dark, gray flat at base

featureless layers
that land meets sea cloud designs
clouds thick sharp rock-gray

hydraulic actions
waves smashing rock-strewn beaches
immense jagged rocks

TANKA POEMS

tanka poetry is an ancient japanese form consisting of five lines, with a traditional syllable count of 5,7,5,7,7. our modern tanka poets don't always follow having the exact 31 syllables. tanka poetry traditionally untitled with minimal punctuation and capitalization which is my favorite favorite part since I do not like to capitalize much at all. about writing in this form compared to writing haiku: tanka poems can use simile, can use metaphor, opinions, and sentiments and even use some rhyme

TANKA POEMS ABOUT THE NIGHT AND THE NIGHT-TIME SKY

say 100 dives
up into the nighttime sky
dark black graceful and so deep
stars sparkle like apartments'
city lights in the evenings

peaceful night time sky
cuddle up all comfortable
snug with a great book
MOON AND STARS PEEKING INSIDE

the winter's breezy
loud tapping on the windows
leafless tree branches
swaying against roof shingles
the bright moon sees me frightened

i shut out my light
and lean on the window sill
my eyes look up in the sky's
blue with illuminations

www.ingramcontent.com/pod-product-compliance
Lightning Source LLC
Chambersburg PA
CBHW072035060426
42449CB00010BA/2269